Daily Wisdom

·

Selections from the
Holy Qur'an

Daily Wisdom

Selections from the
Holy Qur'an

Abdur Raheem Kidwai

KUBE
PUBLISHING

Daily Wisdom: Selections from the Holy Qur'an

First published in England by

Kube Publishing Ltd.
Markfield Conference Centre
Ratby Lane, Markfield,
Leicestershire LE67 9SY
United Kingdom
Tel: +44 (0) 1530 249230
Fax: +44 (0) 1530 249656
Website: www.kubepublishing.com
Email: info@kubepublishing.com

© Abdur Raheem Kidwai, 2011
17th impression, 2023
All rights reserved

The right of Abdur Raheem Kidwai to be
identified as the author of this work has been
asserted by him in accordance with the
Copyright, Designs and Patents Act, 1988.

Cataloguing-in-Publication Data
is available from the British Library

ISBN 978-1-84774-032-8 *casebound*
ISBN 978-1-84774-037-3 *casebound (delux edition with slipcase)*

Book Design & Typesetting: Imtiaz Manjra

Printed by Imak Ofset, Turkey

CONTENTS

PREFACE

This work attempts to set out the meaning and message of the Qur'an in simple, understandable English for the general reader, Muslim and non-Muslim alike. Although there are more than 60 complete English translations of the Qur'an, these are quite often addressed to more specialist readerships. They presuppose some background knowledge of comparative religion, theology, history, geography and of Qur'anic Arabic terms on the part of readers. However, the present work offers a selection of 365 Qur'anic passages for the purpose of daily reflection and study. These passages have been selected to convey the universal and eternal truths and the clear guidance about living a good and ethical life that is to be found in the Qur'an.

Rather than presenting a literal translation of the Qur'an, these passages have been paraphrased in uncomplicated English, while striving to retain its original message. As such, all readers are requested not to judge this work by the strictest standards of literal and accurate translation, as its main aim is to emphasize intelligibility and clarity. I have also drawn heavily upon the following English translations: Abdullah Yusuf Ali's *The Holy Qur'an*, Sayyid Abul Al'a Mawdudi's *Towards Understanding the Qur'an*, and Abdul Majid Daryabadi's *Tafsirul Qur'an: Translation and Commentary of the Holy Qur'an*.

This selection from the Qur'an is meant to be paired with another work of mine, *Daily Wisdom: Sayings of the Prophet Muhammad*, which is also published with Kube; both works will help the general reader to come to a better understanding of the Islamic worldview in its essentials – in its fundamental beliefs, values, morals and teachings.

Finally I would like to thank the team at Kube Publishing in Markfield, England – Haris Ahmad, Yahya Birt and Anwar Cara – for bringing out this work. As always, any suggestions on how to improve future editions would be most welcome.

Abdur Raheem Kidwai
Aligarh Muslim University, India
February 2011

INTRODUCTION

And if you (humanity) are in doubt about what God sent down upon His servant (the Prophet Muhammad) then produce a chapter like it and call your witness or helpers besides God, if you are truthful.

But if you cannot, and certainly you cannot (produce it), then fear the Fire whose fuel is men and stones. Hellfire is prepared for the unbelievers. (Al-Baqarah 2:23-24)

In this quoted passage, the Qur'an presents a clear and cogent account of Scripture – that it is Divine in origin, that it was revealed to the Prophet Muhammad ﷺ, that he faithfully transmitted it to humanity, and that he played no role in its composition. As the bearer of the Qur'an, the role of the Prophet Muhammad ﷺ is essentially as God's servant. In short, the Qur'an affirms that it is wholly the Word of God. Furthermore, the Qur'an declares that it is a unique and inimitable miracle. In stating these articles of faith, the Qur'an aims to dispel all misconceptions about Scripture, which forms the very basis of a faith community – it leaves no room for any confusion.

While its first audience was the seventh-century Arabs, the core ideas in this passage remain timeless and universal:
• The Qur'an is the direct Word of God.

- It was sent down piecemeal to God's servant, the Prophet Muhammad ﷺ.
- The Qur'an is inimitable.
- No human being, individually or jointly, can produce anything like the Qur'an.
- Those refusing these truths about the Qur'an will be consigned to the Hellfire.

Moreover, the passage indicates the Oneness and Omnipotence of God, the exalted prophetic status as well as the humanity of the Prophet Muhammad ﷺ and the genuineness of the Qur'an as the Word of God.

At the outset, it is declared that the Qur'an is the direct Word of God. On this count the Qur'an excels all other existing Scriptures, for they have been altered or misunderstood over time. Indeed even the most exacting scholarship struggles without success to distinguish between their Divine and human components properly. By contrast, the text and meaning of the Qur'an has been preserved since the day of its revelation up to the present day. It remains word for word exactly as it was sent down by God to the Prophet Muhammad ﷺ 14 centuries ago.

Another striking and unique feature of the Qur'an is its gradual revelation, spread out over 23 years. It was sent down as a Book of Guidance to its immediate audience – the seventh-century Arabs – whose often testing circumstances changed dramatically during the course of its revelation. Naturally, this growing community of believers needed that guidance at each and every step; the successful steering of this community in such trying circumstances is confirmation of the Qur'an's status as the Word of God. Upon this foundation of Revelation over 23 years, the message of God's Oneness and the final Prophethood of Muhammad (may God bless and give him peace) spread in a few short decades from the Arabian Peninsula to France in the West to China in the East. Only God's Book could accomplish such a miracle in so a short time; indeed, such a feat is without an historic parallel.

In the above passage, Muhammad ﷺ is described as a servant of God and as a recipient of Revelation: his roles as a servant and as a recipient are emphasized to refute the erroneous misconception that he composed the Qur'an. Being a servant of God he regarded the faithful conveyance of the Qur'an to humanity as his greatest privilege. However, blinded by their stubborn opposition to Islam, the unbelieving Arabs rejected the Qur'an as the product of the Prophet's mind. In this passage they are asked to see reason and realize that the Prophet – as God's obedient servant – did not and could not have ascribed anything to God which was not His. Notwithstanding this weighty argument from the Qur'an, even present-day detractors of Islam persist in making the same groundless charge by dubbing the Qur'an as the work of the Prophet Muhammad ﷺ. It shows their ignorance of the phenomenon of Divine revelation and their inability to note the absolute distinction between the human and the Divine. In their misguided attempt to divest the Qur'an of its Divine origin, they betray their lack of discernment for a work as perfect as the Qur'an could never have been the product of any human mind.

Indeed, the Qur'an throws out an open challenge, daring the unbelievers to compose even one chapter (*surah*) like the Qur'an. They are further told to seek the help of others, including those whom they imagine to be gods besides God in taking up this challenge. As part of this awesome ultimatum, the Qur'an asserts that the unbelievers – both in the present and in the future – will never succeed in meeting this test. History testifies that this Qur'anic challenge has remained unanswered. Instead, humanity should affirm the miraculous nature of the Qur'an and their subservience to God. Given these incontrovertible truths, humanity should not further pursue the path of falsehood or self-destruction which would only land them in Hellfire, for both the unbelievers and their idols made out of stone will be the fuel of Hellfire. It is said that the unbelievers will be anguished to see their idols being roasted in Hellfire alongside themselves. This dire warning rests upon the premise that the Qur'an is an inimitable work: the unbelievers will never be successful in composing anything like the Qur'an because it is characterized by numerous outstanding features. Of these, the following are worth mentioning.

Firstly, unlike the palpable miracles granted to earlier Messengers, which were specific to their time and place, the Qur'an is timeless, and is relevant for all humanity until the end of time.

Secondly, the Qur'an is unmatched in terms of its literary, linguistic and rhetorical excellence, a point conceded, in equal measure, by both the seventh-century unbelieving Arabs and by the twentieth-century Orientalists. Since its revelation, the Qur'an has set the standard in Arabic language and literature, a standard against which all literary works are measured. In its vocabulary, usage, idiom, figurative language, literary devices, narrative techniques, textual finesse and stylistic features the Qur'an is a work *par excellence*. Any human work pales into insignificance in comparison to its literary splendour and majesty.

Thirdly, notwithstanding its considerable length, consisting of more than 6000 verses, the Qur'an stands out for its perfect coherence and cohesion. Unity of thought and singleness of purpose permeate and bind every part of the text. This distinction has never been achieved in any other literary work composed by man. Some Qur'an scholars have conclusively identified this continuity of thought and thematic unity, manifesting itself as it does like a thread, connecting one verse with the next and one chapter with the next. Such thematic links appear to be more pronounced between the concluding part of one chapter and the opening of the next. In sum, the Qur'an is thematically an indivisible whole. Its distinct overarching worldview characterizes each and every part of it. Such amazing unity of thought and dexterity in introducing and developing intertwined themes is unimaginable in any product of the human mind.

Fourthly, the several layers of meaning found in the Qur'an is its other baffling characteristic. Readers of varying mental calibre may grasp the meaning and message of the Qur'an to their utmost satisfaction. Yet on each reading the Qur'an yields new meanings. It would be in vain to look for such remarkable breadth of register or prodigality of meaning in any human work.

Fifthly, the Qur'an is essentially the Book of guidance. In this respect, once again, it is unique. Contained within it are directives of abiding value for individuals in their personal lives and for community and society at large. Within the Qur'an is guidance for every conceivable situation in which a person might find himself – in adversity or prosperity, in war or peace, in fear or hope, and in powerlessness and leadership. In all that the Qur'an relates, especially in the history of earlier communities, the aim of guidance is always to the fore. It is to the Qur'an's credit that its immediate addressees, the seventh-century Arabs who were notorious for their evil ways and moral and spiritual degeneration, were transformed into timeless role models of excellent conduct and enviable morals and manners.

Their transformation, needless to add, was achieved thanks only to the guidance imparted to them by the Qur'an. More tellingly, the Qur'an has continued to provide the same guidance to millions of people in every age, including in our own times. No book can compare in any degree with the Qur'an in terms of the perfect guidance it embodies for everyone – the rich and the poor, the old and the young, the learned and the simple, the ruler and the ruled, and for women and men. As an impeccable code of conduct governing every sphere of life, it instructs humanity comprehensively in how to live their individual lives in the best manner, in a way that will secure their deliverance and will promote peace and happiness in the world. For its vast and comprehensive guidance that benefits every part of society and every kind of human culture the Qur'an ranks as supreme. The Qur'an is fundamentally a universal moral code, which urges humanity to profess and practise good works and to shun evil. It cautions humanity against all that is injurious to its moral, emotional, psychological and spiritual well-being. Its moral precepts infuse human self-restraint, God-consciousness and sincerity in both word and deed. History bears testimony to the fact the Qur'an achieved remarkable success in changing the mind-set of its readers. Unlike any human creation, it is free from any flaws. Neither before nor since the revelation of the Qur'an has any book attained the distinction of bringing about the moral transformation of billions of human souls.

Sixthly, the Qur'anic scheme of things, which embraces life in this world and in the Afterlife, is amazingly vast. It links our present life with our eternal life in the Hereafter. In so doing, it neither rejects life in this world nor the individual's concomitant obligations towards God and towards fellow human beings, whether to his immediate family or to humanity at large. Yet the Qur'an does not ask the individual to divert his mind and let his heart swerve even momentarily from thought of the Afterlife, for the Qur'an condemns materialism. The Qur'an alone holds the distinction of maintaining a fine balance between this life and the concerns of the next. It is beyond the human mind to strike such a perfect amalgam, for the annals of human thought are littered with the extremes of renouncing life altogether or of taking this world as an end in itself.

Seventhly, the Qur'an presents us with the exemplary role model of exemplary human behaviour in both theory and practice. Throughout his illustrious life, the Prophet Muhammad ﷺ exemplified what the Qur'an teaches. On the one hand, the Qur'an provides detailed guidance on every major moral issue, and, on the other, it brings into sharp relief the living examples of historical personalities, both good and evil. At one end of the scale is the inspiring example of the Prophet Noah (peace and blessings be upon him) who preached the Divine message and led a pious life. In sharp contrast to him is his own recalcitrant son who defies God and incurs Divine punishment. Other outstanding examples of vivid juxtaposition are the devout Prophet Abraham (peace and blessings be upon him) and his unbelieving father who was given to idolatry, the transgressing Pharaoh of Egypt and his pious wife, the Prophet Adam (peace and blessings be upon him) and his wicked son; the Prophet Lot (peace and blessings be upon him) and his treacherous wife, and the Prophet Joseph (peace and blessings be upon him) and his jealous brothers. These ever-living examples timelessly instruct humanity: the power of such narratives to inspire us to emulate the God-fearing is not to be found in any work authored by the men of letters.

Eighthly, the Qur'an surpasses all the books in the world for being the most widely-read book in existence. There is no doubt that translations of the Bible are available in most of the world's languages "yet the numbers who go through these in ten years is just a fraction of those who recite the Qur'an every day".[1] Notwithstanding the intensively hostile and negative propaganda against the Qur'an carried out by polemicists of all hues, the popularity of the Qur'an has gown phenomenally with the passage of time. For well over a billion people it is the most scared work on earth and their devotion to it is impressive. The respect and devotion inspired by the Qur'an is unimaginable for any human enterprise. It is common knowledge that works paraded as original, groundbreaking and seminal grow become outdated in short measure. The Qur'an has, however, retained its pivotal position among Muslims to the present day.

Ninthly and finally, the preservation of the Qur'an for more than 1400 years establishes, once again, its Divine credentials, which are not shared by any measure with any other book. That the Qur'an has remained intact even after 14 centuries is acknowledged even by the Orientalists, "It is an immense merit in the Qur'an that there is no doubt as to its genuineness. That very word we can now read with

---

1. Sayyid Abul Hasan Ali Nadwi, "Introduction", *The Glorious Qur'an*, translated by 'Abdul Majid Daryabadi (Markfield, UK: Islamic Foundation, 2002), pp. xx-xxi.

full confidence that it has remained unchanged though nearly thirteen hundred years." Or, "There is probably in the world no other work [except the Qur'an] which has remained twelve centuries with so pure a text."[2] The continuous practice of Qur'an memorization by countless numbers of Muslims from one generation to the next has guaranteed the perfect preservation of the text: no other book can match such an error-free arrangement for its safeguarding.

For all these reasons and more, the present selection introduces readers to the Holy Qur'an, and provides an opening and an opportunity to study, reflect upon and assimilate this enduring and universal message. It is to be hoped that this selection encourages further and deeper study of the Book of God, which is the deeply rewarding endeavour of a lifetime.

---

2. Respectively, Stanley Lane-Poole, *Selections from the Qur'an* (Boston, 1879), p.3; William Muir, *Life of Muhammad* (London, 1856), p. xxii.

Daily Wisdom

Selections from the
Holy Qur'an

DAY 1

O human beings, God has created all of you from a male and a female, and made you into nations and tribes so that you may recognize one another. However, the best among you in the sight of God is the one who is the most pious. God is All-Knowing, All-Wise.

Al-Hujurat 49:13

DAY
2

orship no one other than God; be good to your parents and relatives, and to the orphan and the poor. Speak kindly to everyone, establish Prayer and give in charity (*Zakah*).

Al-Baqarah 2:83

ح o God belongs the east and the west.
So wherever you turn, in fact you turn to
God. God is All-Embracing, All-Knowing.

Al-Baqarah 2:115

DAY
4

Do not confound the truth by mixing it up with falsehood and do not knowingly conceal the truth.

Al-Baqarah 2:42

DAY
5

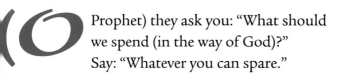

Prophet) they ask you: "What should
we spend (in the way of God)?"
Say: "Whatever you can spare."

Al-Baqarah 2:219

Τ here are signs for people who use their reason,

In the creation of the heavens and the earth,

In the alternation of day and night,

In the ships that sail on the sea, carrying goods that are of profit to humanity,

In the water that God sends from the heavens, which revives the earth after its death,

In the scattering of all kinds of animals,

In the changing courses of the winds and the clouds pressed into service between the heavens and the earth.

Al-Baqarah 2:164

God! There is no god except Him, the Ever-Living, the Self-Subsisting. Neither slumber nor sleep overtakes Him. His is whatever is in the heavens and whatever is on earth. Who is there who can intercede with Him, except by His permission? He knows what is in front of people and what is behind them. But they cannot encompass anything of God's knowledge except what He wills. His authority extends over the heavens and the earth and their guarding does not tire Him. He is Most-High, All-Glorious.

Al-Baqarah 2:255

Those who spend their wealth in the way of God and then do not follow up their spending by taunting or causing hurt (to others) – they will find their reward with God. They have no cause to fear or grieve.

Al-Baqarah 2:262

DAY
9

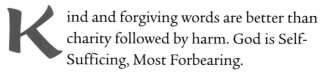

Kind and forgiving words are better than charity followed by harm. God is Self-Sufficing, Most Forbearing.

Al-Baqarah 2:263

D o not waste your acts of charity by reminders of your generosity or causing harm, as does he who spends his wealth only to be seen by people, and does not believe in God and the Last Day.

The example of his spending is that of a rock with dust on it: when the heavy rain falls, it leaves the rock bare. Such people gain nothing from their charity. God does not guide those who refuse to accept the truth.

Al-Baqarah 2:264

DAY
11

God does not force anyone to do beyond what is within his capacity. Everyone will get the reward he earns and will be responsible for the evil he does.

Al-Baqarah 2:286

n the Day of Judgement every soul will be confronted with whatever good and evil it has done. It will then wish there was a great distance between itself and the Day of Judgement. God warns you to beware of Him. He is Most Kind to His servants.

Al 'Imran 3:30

DAY
13

nd race to seek forgiveness from your Lord and towards Paradise which is as vast as the heaven and the earth, and which is prepared

For those who fear God,

For those who are generous in both good and bad times,

For those who control (their) anger and pardon people. God loves those who do good,

And those who remember God and ask forgiveness for their sins when they do some evil or wrong their souls.

Who can forgive sins but God? »

« They do not knowingly persist in the wrong they have done.

Their reward is forgiveness from their Lord, and the gardens in Paradise beneath which rivers flow.

There they shall abide. How good is the reward of those who sincerely do good!

Al 'Imran 3:133-136

DAY
14

People! Fear your Lord Who created you from a single being and out of it created its mate; and out of the two spread numerous men and women. Fear God in Whose name you demand rights and be careful about the ties of relationships. Surely God is Ever Watchful over you.

Al-Nisa' 4:1-2

est the orphans until they reach the age of marriage and then if you find them mature of mind, hand their property over to them, and do not devour it by either spending it wastefully or in haste, fearing that they would grow up (and claim it). If the guardian of the orphan is rich, let him take nothing from it and if he is poor, let him take from it in a fair way. When you hand over their property to them, call in witnesses in their presence. God is sufficient to take account (of your works).

Al-Nisa' 4:6

od commands justice, kindness and doing good to relatives, and forbids all shameful acts, injustice and wrongdoing. He instructs you thus so that you may pay due attention.

Al-Nahl 16:90

o not covet what God has granted more abundantly on some of you than on others. Men will have a portion of what they earn and women will have a portion of what they earn. Do ask God for His bounty. God knows everything.

Al-Nisa' 4:32

erve God and do not ascribe any partner to Him. Do good to your parents and relatives, to orphans and to the needy, and to the neighbour who is your relative and to the neighbour who is a stranger, to the companion by your side, and to the traveller and to those whom your right hands possess. God does not love the arrogant, the boastful.

Al-Nisa' 4:36

 ay: "He is God, the One and Unique. God is not in need of anyone while everyone is in need of Him. He neither gives birth nor is He born. No one is comparable to Him."

Al-Ikhlas 112:1-4

DAY
20

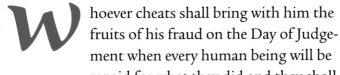

hoever cheats shall bring with him the fruits of his fraud on the Day of Judgement when every human being will be repaid for what they did and they shall not be wronged in the least.

Al 'Imran 3:161

DAY
21

hoever does good and has faith – whether male or female – shall enter Paradise and they shall not be wronged in the slightest.

Al-Nisa' 4:124

DAY
22

urely it is God Who causes the seed and the date-stone to sprout. He brings forth the living from the dead and the dead from the living. Such is God! So why then do you persist in error?

Al-An'am 6:95

nd when it is said to them: "Spend (in the way of God) out of the sustenance which God has provided you," the unbelievers say to the believers: "Shall we feed him whom God would have fed, had He so wished?" Say: "You are clearly in error."

Ya' Sin 36:47

DAY
24

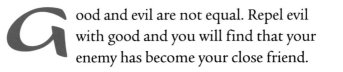

ood and evil are not equal. Repel evil with good and you will find that your enemy has become your close friend.

Ha'. Mim. Al-Sajdah 41:34

 children of Adam! God has given garments to you in order to hide your shame – and as adornment for you. But the finest of all is the garment of piety. That is one of the signs of God so that people may take heed.

Al-A'raf 7:26

It is God Who has made the earth a dwelling place for you and made the sky a canopy. He has shaped you, and shaped you well and given you good things as sustenance. Such is God, your Lord! Blessed is God, the Lord of the universe! He is the Ever-Living: there is no god other than Him. So turn to Him sincerely, having faith only in Him. Praise be to God, the Lord of the universe.

Al-Mu'min 40:64-65

DAY
27

 very living being shall taste death. God
will test you with good and evil, and to
Him you will return.

Al-Anbiya' 21:35

DAY
28

od is the light of the heavens and the earth. His light may be likened to a niche in which there is a lamp; the lamp is in a crystal as though it is a shining star, lit from a blessed olive tree, neither of the east nor of the west, whose oil glows forth even though no fire has touched it. Light upon light! God guides to this light those whom He wills.

Al-Nur 24:35

DAY
29

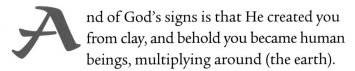

nd of God's signs is that He created you
from clay, and behold you became human
beings, multiplying around (the earth).

Al-Rum 30:20

DAY
30

od has commanded man to be kind to his parents. In pain did his mother bear him and in pain did she give birth to him. The carrying of the child up to his weaning is a period of thirty months.

Al-Ahqaf 46:15

 people, consider this parable: Those upon whom you call, besides God, cannot create (even) a fly, if they all met together for that purpose. And if the fly snatches away anything from them, they would not be able to recover that from it. Powerless are those who call and those called (upon)!

Al-Hajj 22:73

ive to your close relative his due and also
to the needy and the traveller.

Bani Isra'il 17:26

Cooperate with one another in doing good and piety and do not help one another in sin and rebellion (against God).

Al-Ma'idah 5:2

DAY
34

 o give the near of kin his due, and to the needy and the traveller. That is best for those who want to have God's pleasure. It is they who will prosper.

Al-Rum 30:38

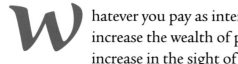hatever you pay as interest so that it may increase the wealth of people does not increase in the sight of God. But what you give in charity, seeking God's pleasure, will increase many times.

Al-Rum 30:39

DAY
36

God is He Who created you in a state of weakness (as a baby); then after weakness He gave you strength; then after strength He made you weak and old. He creates what He wills. He is All-Knowing, All-Powerful.

Al-Rum 30:54

DAY
37

urely those who believe and do good works shall have gardens of bliss (in Paradise). They shall live in them forever. This is God's promise that shall come true. He is All-Powerful, All-Wise.

Luqman 31:8-9

God has commanded man to be dutiful to his parents. His mother bore him in hardship upon hardship, and his weaning lasted two years. (God, therefore, commands:) "Give thanks to Me and to your parents. To Me is your ultimate return."

Luqman 31:14

 people! Fear your Lord and dread the Day when no father will stand for his child. Nor will any child stand for his father. Surely God's promise is true. So let not the life of this world deceive you and let not the deceiver (Satan) deceive you about God.

Luqman 31:33

DAY
40

It is by neither your wealth nor your children that you are brought nearer to God: only he who believes and does good works; it is they who will receive a double reward for their acts. They shall live in lofty mansions of Paradise in perfect peace.

Saba' 34:37

urely those who give charity, be they men or women, give God a beautiful loan and they shall be repaid after increasing it many times. They shall have a generous reward.

Al-Hadid 57:18

DAY
42

 believers, fear God and believe in His Messenger, and He will grant you a double portion of His mercy, and provide you with a light by which you shall walk, and He will forgive you. God is Most Forgiving, Most Merciful.

Al-Hadid 57:28

D o you observe him who denies the Day of Judgement? He is the one who snubs the orphan and does not encourage feeding the poor. Woe to those who pray without paying attention to their prayers; those who do good only to be seen, and who deny people common kindnesses!

Al-Ma'un 107:1-7

DAY
44

God is the Originator of the heavens and the earth. When He decides something, He (only) says to it: "Be" and it is.

Al-Baqarah 2:117

DAY
45

Prophet) when My servants ask you about Me, tell them I am near; I hear and answer the call of every caller whenever he calls me. Ask them to listen to My message and believe in Me. They will perhaps then be guided to the right path.

Al-Baqarah 2:186

DAY
46

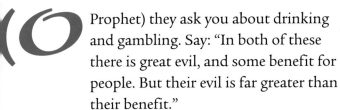

Prophet) they ask you about drinking and gambling. Say: "In both of these there is great evil, and some benefit for people. But their evil is far greater than their benefit."

Al-Baqarah 2:219

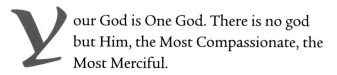

Your God is One God. There is no god but Him, the Most Compassionate, the Most Merciful.

Al-Baqarah 2:163

here is no compulsion in religion. The right way stands clearly distinct from the wrong way. So he who rejects the evil ones and believes in God has indeed taken hold of the firm, unbreakable handle. God is All-Hearing, All-Knowing.

Al-Baqarah 2:256

I f you give charity publicly, it is good.
But if you conceal it and pay it privately
to the needy, it is better for you. This will
compensate for some of your evil acts.
And God is fully aware of all that you do.

Al-Baqarah 2:271

DAY
50

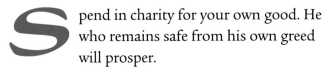

Spend in charity for your own good. He who remains safe from his own greed will prosper.

Al-Taghabun 64:16

God does not wrong anyone at all. When one does good, God doubles it and out of His grace gives a great reward.

Al-Nisa' 4:40

DAY
52

He who does good shall have ten times as much to his credit. However, he who does wrong shall be repaid according to its equivalent.

Al-An'am 6:160

DAY
53

od has created you and then causes you to die. Some of you have your life up to a weak, old age, when you lose all knowledge after having acquired it. God is All-Knowing, All-Powerful.

Al-Nahl 16:70

hose who devour the property of orphans, they fill their bellies with fire. Soon they will roast in the blazing fire (of Hell).

Al-Nisa' 4:10

If you take revenge, then do so only in proportion to the wrong done to you. But if you bear it patiently, that is indeed best for those who are patient.

Al-Nahl 16:126

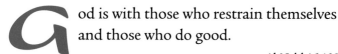

od is with those who restrain themselves
and those who do good.

Al-Nahl 16:128

He who follows guidance does so for his own benefit, and he who goes astray does so to his own loss. No one shall bear another's burden.

Bani Isra'il 17:15

our Lord has commanded that you worship none but Him, and that you be kind to your parents. Should either or both of them attain old age with you, do not say to them a word of contempt nor repel them, but speak to them with respect, and be humble and kind to them and say: "Lord, have mercy on them as they brought me up when I was young."

Bani Isra'il 17:23-24

od shall set up scales of justice on the Day of Judgement. No one will be wronged there in the least. God shall bring to account the acts of everyone, even if it may be equal to the weight of a mustard seed. God is sufficient to bring everyone to account.

Al-Anbiya' 21:47

he true servants of the Merciful God are those who walk on the earth in humility and when the ignorant people address them, they reply: "Peace be upon you."

Al-Furqan 25:63

DAY
61

God knows what goes into the earth and what comes forth from it; what comes down from the heavens and what goes up to it. He is All-Merciful, All-Forgiving.

Saba' 34:2

DAY
62

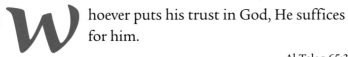

Whoever puts his trust in God, He suffices for him.

Al-Talaq 65:3

God makes the dawn break and has made the night for rest, and the sun and the moon for measuring (time). This is the arrangement of the Almighty, the All-Knowing.

Al-An'am 6:96

DAY
64

hen man suffers some trouble, he cries out to God but when God grants him a favour, he says: "I have been given this on account of my knowledge." No, it is but a trial but most of them do not realize that.

Al-Zumar 39:49

It is God Who has made for you the stars that you may follow the right direction in the darkness of the land and the sea. God has explained the signs for people who understand.

Al-An'am 6:97

The repaying of an injury is injury in an equal degree. However, he who forgives and makes reconciliation, his reward is with God. God does not love those who do wrong.

Al-Shura 42:40

The unbelievers say: "There is no life except the life of this world. We live and die and it is only time that destroys us." But they do not have any true knowledge. They merely speculate.

Al-Jathiyah 45:24

mong God's signs is that He has created spouses for you of your own kind for you to live with in peace. He has put love and kindness between you. Surely these are signs for those who reflect.

Al-Rum 30:21

Fear the Day of Judgement when no one will help another: when no intercession will be accepted, when no compensation will be taken, and when no one will be helped.

Al-Baqarah 2:48

DAY
70

elievers, avoid suspicion as much as possible. For suspicion in some cases is a sin. Do not spy on one another, nor speak ill of them behind their backs. Would any of you like to eat the flesh of your dead brother? No, you would abhor it. So fear God: God is ever ready to accept repentance and is Most Merciful.

Al-Hujurat 49:12

elievers, let not a group of men laugh at another group. It may be that they are better than those (laughing at them). Nor let a group of women laugh at another group. It may be that they are better than those (laughing at them). Do not taunt one another nor call one another by offensive nicknames.

Al-Hujurat 49:11

DAY
72

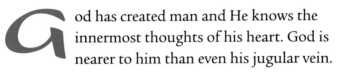

God has created man and He knows the innermost thoughts of his heart. God is nearer to him than even his jugular vein.

Qaf 50:16

It is God Who sends the winds as bearers, announcing His mercy. Then He sends down pure water from the sky that He may bring life to dead land and let His creation – cattle and men – drink from it. He presents this wonderful scene before them over and again so that they may learn a lesson from it. But most of the people refuse (to do) anything except disbelieve in it.

Al-Furqan 25:50

God will unite the believers with those of their children who followed them in their faith and will not deny them any part of the reward for their good deeds. Everyone will be rewarded or punished according to their deeds.

Al-Tur 52:21

It is the Merciful God Who taught the Qur'an. He has created man and has taught him speech. The sun and the moon follow their respective courses and the stars and trees all bow in adoration (to God). He has raised up the heaven and has set us the balance (of justice) so that you may not deviate and weigh things fairly and not fall short in the balance. He has set down the earth for all his creatures.

Al-Rahman 55:1-10

DAY
76

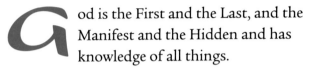

od is the First and the Last, and the
Manifest and the Hidden and has
knowledge of all things.

Al-Hadid 57:3

ell believing men to lower their gaze and
guard their private parts. That is purer
for them. God is well aware of all that
they do.

Tell believing women to lower their gaze
and guard their private parts, and not to
display their charms except what nor-
mally appears of them.

Al-Nur 24:30-31

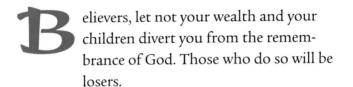

Believers, let not your wealth and your children divert you from the remembrance of God. Those who do so will be losers.

Al-Munafiqun 63:9

pend (in charity) out of the things God has given you before death overtakes you and you say: "My Lord, if you would reprieve me for a while so that I might give charity and do good?"

God does not give a soul respite when its time comes. God is completely aware of all that you do.

Al-Munafiqun 63:10-11

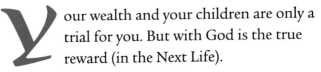

Your wealth and your children are only a trial for you. But with God is the true reward (in the Next Life).

Al-Taghabun 64:15

DAY
81

ou cannot become a truly pious person unless you spend (for the sake of God) out of what you love. God knows all that you spend.

Al 'Imran 3:92

Let the rich spend in charity according to their capacity and they who have limited resources, let them spend according to what God has given them. God does not burden anyone beyond what He has given him. God will grant ease after difficulty.

Al-Talaq 65:7

God has made the earth manageable for you so that you may walk about its regions and earn the sustenance that He has provided. To Him will you be returned.

Al-Mulk 67:15

那hose who are trustworthy and keep their promises, those who are fair in their testimony, those who take due care of their Prayer, they shall be the honoured ones in the gardens of Paradise.

Al-Ma'arij 70:32-35

For the love of God they (the pious) feed the needy, the orphan and the captive, saying: "We feed you for the sake of God alone. We do not seek any reward or thanks from you."

Al-Dahr 76:8-9

DAY
86

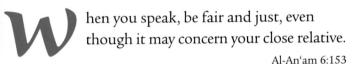

When you speak, be fair and just, even
though it may concern your close relative.

Al-An'am 6:153

o they not observe the camels: how they are created? And the sky: how it is raised high? And the mountains: how they are fixed? And the earth: how it is spread out?

Al-Ghashiyah 88:17-20

DAY
88

In God's Messenger (the Prophet Muhammad) there is an excellent example for you and for all those who look forward to (meeting) God and the Last Day and who remember God much.

Al-Ahzab 33:21

oe to him who engages in slander and backbiting, who amasses wealth and counts it over and over again, thinking that his wealth will make him immortal. Indeed, no, he shall be thrust into crushing torment.

Al-Humazah 104:1-4

od commands you to return what you safeguard to its owners. When you judge between people, judge fairly. Excellent people judge with justice. Excellent is the advice that God gives you. God is All-Hearing, All-Seeing.

Al-Nisa' 4:58

D o they not reflect on the Qur'an? Had it come from other than God, they would have found much contradiction in it.

Al-Nisa' 4:82

DAY
92

od has given you the faculties of hearing, sight and intellect. Yet you give little thanks. He has dispersed you all over the earth, and to Him you shall be brought back. He gives you life and causes death and He controls the alternation of night and day. Do you not reflect?

Al-Mu'minun 23: 78-80

DAY
93

God does not forgive that a partner be associated with Him, although He forgives any other sin for whom He wills. He who takes anyone as a partner with God indeed lies and has committed a great sin.

Al-Nisa' 4:48

DAY
94

o not you see how your Lord lengthens the shadow? Had He willed, He could make it stand still. Instead, He has made the sun its pilot. So (as the sun rises), He gradually rolls up the shadow towards Himself. It is God Who has made the night a covering for you and sleep for rest, and makes every (new) day a resurrection.

Al-Furqan 25:45-47

s for those who fear God, they shall be in the gardens and fountains (of Paradise), happily enjoying what their Lord will give them because of the good they had done before – they used to sleep little at night and asked for God's forgiveness at dawn and gave a rightful share of their wealth to the beggar and to the poor.

Al-Dhariyat 51:15-19

DAY
96

od is the One Who accepts repentance from His servants and overlooks (their) evil acts. He knows everything that you do.

Al-Shura 42:25

He who does evil or wrongs himself, and then asks for God's forgiveness will find God All-Forgiving, All-Merciful. He who does a sin, he wrongs his own soul. God is All-Knowing, All-Wise.

Al-Nisa' 4:110-111

*J*f you fear separation between a man and his wife, appoint an arbitrator from his family and another from her family. If they both want to set things right, God will bring about reconciliation between them. God is All-Knowing, All-Aware.

Al-Nisa' 4:35

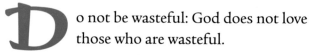

Do not be wasteful: God does not love those who are wasteful.

Al-An'am 6:141

DAY
100

children of Adam! Dress well at every time and place of worship. And eat and drink but do not be wasteful. God does not love the wasters.

Al-A'raf 7:31

ll that is hidden in the heavens and the earth lies within the power of God. To Him are all matters referred for judgement. So serve Him and put your trust in Him. Your Lord is not unaware of what you do.

Hud 11:123

 Believers! Wine, gambling, idols and divining arrows are only a dirty work of Satan. Avoid them wholly so that you may gain true success. Satan only wants to sow enmity and hate among you by wine and gambling and to turn you away from remembering God and from praying. So will you stop (doing wrong)?

Al-Ma'idah 5:90-91

mong the signs of God is the creation of the heavens and the earth and the variety of your languages and colours. Surely there are signs in this for people gifted with knowledge.

Al-Rum 30:22

od created man from an extract of clay. Then He placed him as a drop of semen in a safe resting place. Then He turned the semen into a clot. Next He turned the clot into a tissue and then He turned the tissue into bones and clothed bones with flesh. Thus He made it a new creation. Blessed be God, the best to create!

Al-Mu'minun 23:12-14

In the beginning humanity followed one straight way. (Later on this ended and differences arose.) So God sent Prophets as bearers of good news for the pious and as warners against the consequences of doing evil. He sent them with the Book, containing the truth so that it might decide disputes among humanity.

Al-Baqarah 2:213

DAY
106

od has revealed a Book to you (O Prophet) that you may bring people out of darkness into light and direct them, with the permission of their Lord, to the way of the All-Powerful, Most Praiseworthy.

Ibrahim 14:1

uhammad is not the father of any man among you; He is the Messenger of God and the seal of the Prophets. God is aware of everything.

Al-Ahzab 33:40

Those who spend their wealth day and night (in God's way), both privately and publicly, will find that their reward is secure with their Lord and that there is no reason for them to have any fear or grief.

Al-Baqarah 2:274

He who gives in charity, fears God and does good, God shall make easy for him the path to success. But he who is a greedy miser and thinks himself self-sufficient and does not do good, God will direct him to the path to misery. His wealth will be of no help to him when he dies.

Al-Layl 92:5-11

ay to them (O Prophet): "Come, let me tell you what your Lord has commanded you:

Do not associate anyone with God as His partner;

Be good to your parents;

Do not kill your children out of fear of poverty. God provides for you and will also provide for them;

Do not even go near shameful acts, be they open or secret;

Do not kill any person, the soul sanctified by God except through (the due process of) law. He has instructed you in this so that you may reflect; »

« Do not approach an orphan's wealth before he comes of age, except to improve it;

Give full measure and weight in all fairness. God does not burden any person beyond his capacity.

When you speak, be just and fair, even though it may concern your close relative.

Fulfil your pledge to God. This is what He has instructed you so that you may take it to heart.

Al-An'am 6:151-152

ll that has been given you is only the brief enjoyment of this world. But what is with God is far better and long lasting for those who believe and put their trust in their Lord. They keep away from major sins and shameful acts and forgive when they get angry. They obey their Lord and establish Prayer. They conduct their affairs through consultation among themselves and spend out of what God has provided them. When a wrong is done to them, they seek its remedy.

Al-Shura 42:36-39

"O contented soul! Return to your Lord well pleased (with your happy end), and well pleasing (to your Lord)." (God will tell that soul:) "Join My servants and enter My Paradise."

Al-Fajr 89:27-30

hose who recite God's Book, are constant in Prayer and spend both publicly and privately out of what God has given them, they look forward to a trade that shall suffer no loss. God will repay them their reward and give them even more out of His bounty. He is Most Forgiving, Most Appreciative.

Fatir 35:29-30

Virtue does not mean that you turn your faces to the east or the west. But virtuous is he who believes in God, the Day of Judgement, the angels, the Divine Book and the Messengers; and gives away his wealth, no matter how much he loves it, to his close relatives, orphans, the needy, travellers, beggars and in freeing captives. Virtue means to establish Prayer and pay Charity (*Zakah*), to keep a promise when it is made, to be patient in suffering, hardship and times of violence. They are the ones who have proved true and they are the God-fearing ones.

Al-Baqarah 2:177

DAY
115

Believers, uphold justice, bearing truthful witness before God even though it may be against yourselves, your parents or your close relatives. Whether it may concern (the cases of) the rich or the poor, God is closer to both (than you are). Do not follow your own passions so that you may act justly. If you distort (justice) or turn away (from it), God is aware of what you do.

Al-Nisa' 4:135

Those who keep their trusts and pledges and who are particular about their prayers shall inherit Paradise and remain there for ever.

Al-Mu'minun 23:8-10

od has sent the Messengers with clear signs, and sent the Divine Book and the criterion along with them so that humanity may conduct itself with fairness.

Al-Hadid 57:25

Let man consider his food (and how God provides it): God poured water in plenty, and split the soil into parts, then caused the grain to grow out of it – grapes, vegetables, olives, palms, dense orchards, fruits and pasture – for your use and convenience and of your cattle.

'Abasa 80:24-32

Those who act kindly will have a good reward and even more. Neither darkness nor disgrace will cover their faces (in the Hereafter). They will be the people of Paradise and will remain there forever.

Yunus 10:26

DAY
120

Messenger (Prophet Muhammad) has come to you from among you, who is pained by your losses. He sincerely desires your welfare and is kind and merciful towards the believers.

Al-Tawbah 9:128

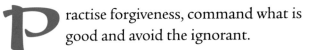

ractise forgiveness, command what is good and avoid the ignorant.

Al-A'raf 7:199

DAY 122

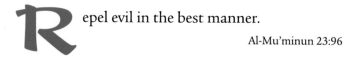

Repel evil in the best manner.

Al-Mu'minun 23:96

D o not turn your face away with contempt from people and do not walk arrogantly upon the earth. God neither loves the arrogant nor the boastful.

Luqman 31:18

od does not forbid you to deal kindly and justly with those who have not fought against you on account of religion nor expelled you from your homes. God loves those who are just.

Al-Mumtahinah 60:8

elievers, do not enter houses other than your own until you have obtained permission from their residents and greeted them politely. This is better for you. It is expected that you will observe this ... And if you are told to go away, then do so: it is more fitting for you. God is aware of everything you do.

Al-Nur 24:27-28

If God were to punish people according to what they deserved, He would not leave a single creature on the face of the earth. However, He grants them respite for an appointed term, but when that term ends – surely God has been watching His servants.

Fatir 35:45

DAY
127

mong the signs of God is that He shows
you lightning that arouses both fear and
hope. And God sends down rain from
the sky and with it gives life to the earth
after it is dead. Surely there are signs in
this for those who reflect.

Al-Rum 30:24

 God, Lord of power! You give power to whom You please and You take it away from whom You please. You honour whom You please and humble whom You please. In Your hand is all good. Over all things You have power. You merge night into day and day into night. You draw the living from the dead and the dead from the living. You give sustenance without measure to whom You will.

Al 'Imran 3:26-27

DAY
129

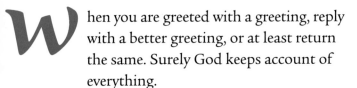

When you are greeted with a greeting, reply with a better greeting, or at least return the same. Surely God keeps account of everything.

Al-Nisa' 4:86

 Believers! When a wicked person brings to you some news, carefully verify its truth lest you harm people out of ignorance and then regret what you did.

Al-Hujurat 49:6

Your Lord inspired the bee: "Make your home in the hills, in the trees and in (men's) habitations, then feed on every kind of fruit and follow the paths made easy for you by your Lord." There comes forth from their bellies a drink (honey), varied in colour, in which there is healing for people. Surely there is a sign in it for those who reflect.

Al-Nahl 16:68-69

DAY
132

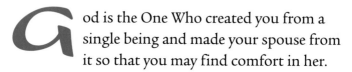

od is the One Who created you from a single being and made your spouse from it so that you may find comfort in her.

Al-A'raf 7:189

From the wealth of the pious the beggar and the poor get their due.

Al-Dhariyat 51:19

Prophet) tell them: "My servants who have wronged themselves should not despair of God's mercy. Turn to your Lord and surrender yourselves to Him before punishment overtakes you. For then you will not receive any help."

Al-Zumar 39:53-54

Prophet) people ask you what they should spend, say: "Whatever money you spend, let it be on your parents and close relatives, orphans, the needy and the traveller. God is aware of all good that you do."

Al-Baqarah 2:215

DAY
136

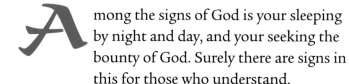mong the signs of God is your sleeping by night and day, and your seeking the bounty of God. Surely there are signs in this for those who understand.

Al-Rum 30:23

Your Lord has prescribed for Himself (the rule of) mercy. If any of you does an evil act out of ignorance and then repents and makes amends, you will surely find God All-Forgiving, Most Merciful.

Al-An'am 6:54

Believers! It is not lawful for you to become heirs to women against their will. It is not lawful that you should put restrictions upon them so that you may take away anything of what you have given them. (You may not put any restrictions upon them) unless they are guilty of openly immoral conduct.

Treat your wives gracefully. If you dislike them in any manner, it may be that you dislike something in which God has placed much good for you.

Al-Nisa' 4:19

o not take one another's belongings by false means. Do not try to bribe authorities with your wealth so that you may sinfully and knowingly take away a portion of someone's belongings.

Al-Baqarah 2:188

DAY
140

If one of you entrusts (something to) another, then let the one who is trusted discharge his trust, and fear God, the Lord. Do not conceal what you witness. Do not hold back testimony: anyone who does so has a sinful heart. God knows all that you do.

Al-Baqarah 2:283

s for those who devour interest, they behave as if Satan has turned them crazy with his touch. Seized in this state they claim: "Buying and selling is a kind of interest," while God has made buying and selling lawful, and interest unlawful.

Al-Baqarah 2:275

Prophet) tell those who hoard gold and silver and do not spend it in the way of God that they will have a painful punishment.

Al-Tawbah 9:34

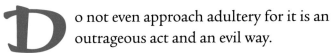

o not even approach adultery for it is an outrageous act and an evil way.

Bani Isra'il 17:32

DAY 144

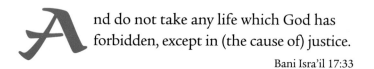

nd do not take any life which God has
forbidden, except in (the cause of) justice.

Bani Isra'il 17:33

DAY 145

Let there be a group among you to call people to all that is good, command what is proper and forbid what is improper. They shall achieve true success.

Al 'Imran 3:104

DAY 146

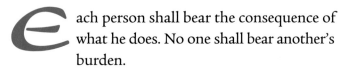

ach person shall bear the consequence of what he does. No one shall bear another's burden.

Al-An'am 6:164

DAY
147

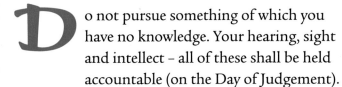

o not pursue something of which you have no knowledge. Your hearing, sight and intellect – all of these shall be held accountable (on the Day of Judgement).

Bani Isra'il 17:36

o not squander your wealth wastefully. Those who squander excessively are brothers of Satan and Satan is ever ungrateful to His Lord.

Bani Isra'il 17:26-27

Do not kill your children for fear of poverty – God will provide for them and for you – killing them is a great sin.

Bani Isra'il 17:31

DAY
150

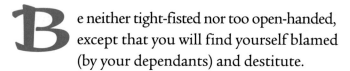

e neither tight-fisted nor too open-handed,
except that you will find yourself blamed
(by your dependants) and destitute.

Bani Isra'il 17:29

DAY
151

Fulfil your pledges, for you will be held accountable (by God) regarding your pledges.

Bani Isra'il 17:34

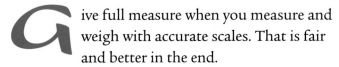

ive full measure when you measure and weigh with accurate scales. That is fair and better in the end.

Bani Isra'il 17:35

Honour the pledge that you have made with God and do not break your oaths after you have taken them and made God your witness (to them). Surely God knows all that you do.

Al-Nahl 16:91

Do not let the hatred of any people lead you to deviate from justice. Act justly: this is what it means to be God-fearing. Be mindful of God alone, for surely God is aware of all that you do.

Al-Ma'idah 5:8

$\int$ s there any reward for kindness other
than kindness itself?

Al-Rahman 55:60

DAY
156

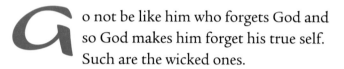

Go not be like him who forgets God and so God makes him forget his true self. Such are the wicked ones.

Al-Hashr 59:19

Prophet Muhammad) say: "I am no more than a human being like you, to whom it has been revealed that your Lord is the One and Only God. So whoever looks forward to meeting his Lord, let him do good and not associate anyone in the worship of his Lord."

Al-Kahf 18:110

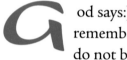 od says:) "Remember Me and I shall remember you. Give thanks to Me and do not be ungrateful to Me for My favours."

Al-Baqarah 2:152

DAY
159

o not give (in charity) expecting a worldly increase.

Al-Muddaththir 74:6

Prayer forbids shameful and evil acts, and the remembrance of God is greater. And God knows all that you do.

Al-'Ankabut 29:45

DAY
161

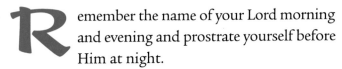

emember the name of your Lord morning and evening and prostrate yourself before Him at night.

Al-Dahr 76:25-26

DAY 162

hen some harm touches man, he cries out to God, reclining, sitting and standing. But no sooner has God removed his difficulty, he passes on as though he had never cried out to God to remove his difficulty. Thus are the evil acts of wicked people made pleasing to them.

Yunus 10:12

DAY
163

To God is your return, and He has power over everything.

Hud 11:4

(T hey are) those who have been driven from their homes without just cause for saying "Our Lord is God". Had it not been that God repels some people through others, monasteries, churches, synagogues and mosques in which the name of God is frequently mentioned would most certainly have been pulled down. God aids those who help His cause, and surely God is Most Powerful, Almighty.

Al-Hajj 22:40

DAY
165

 Believers! Spend (in charity) out of what God has given you before the Day (of Judgement) when there will be no buying or selling, no friendship or inter-cession.

Al-Baqarah 2:254

DAY
166

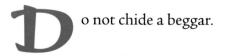

Do not chide a beggar.

Al-Duha 93:10

DAY 167

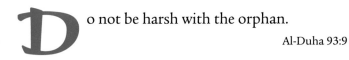

o not be harsh with the orphan.

Al-Duha 93:9

Proclaim and celebrate the bounties of your Lord.

Al-Duha 93:11

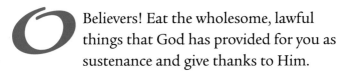

Believers! Eat the wholesome, lawful things that God has provided for you as sustenance and give thanks to Him.

Al-Baqarah 2:172

How many are the creatures that do not carry their sustenance. Yet God provides sustenance for them and for you. He is All-Hearing, All-Knowing.

Al-'Ankabut 29:60

eturn to the orphans their property (when they come of age) and do not exchange your bad things for their good ones. And do not devour their property by mixing it up with your own. This is surely a major sin.

Al-Nisa' 4:2

DAY
172

eek the abode of the Hereafter by wealth that God has given you while not forgetting your own share in this world, and do good (to others) as God has been good to you and do not create mischief in the land. God does not love those who create mischief.

Al-Qasas 28:77

Give women their bridal gift happily, but if they willingly give back part of it, then enjoy it with good pleasure.

Al-Nisa' 4:4

DAY
174

eat and drink of the sustenance provided by God, but do not act wickedly on earth, spreading mischief.

Al-Baqarah 2:60

Prophet) tell people: "My Lord has forbidden all shameful acts, whether done openly or in secret, sins of all kinds and wrongful oppression."

Al-A'raf 7:33

D o not incline towards wrongdoers lest Hellfire seize you and then you will not have anyone to protect you against God and you will not be helped by anyone.

Hud 11:113

 o you ask people to be pious while you do not practise it yourselves, and even though you recite the Book? Have you no sense?

Al-Baqarah 2:44

 Prophet) tell people: "My Lord commands justice."

Al-A'raf 7:29

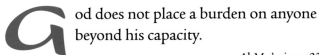

God does not place a burden on anyone beyond his capacity.

Al-Mu'minun 23:62

D o not plead for those who are dishonest
with themselves. God does not love
those who are treacherous and sinful.

Al-Nisa' 4:107

Believers! Do not be unfaithful to God and the Messenger. Do not knowingly betray your trusts. Know well that your belongings and your children are a trial and that there lies a great reward with God.

Al-Anfal 8:27-28

DAY
182

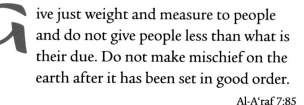

Give just weight and measure to people and do not give people less than what is their due. Do not make mischief on the earth after it has been set in good order.

Al-A'raf 7:85

DAY
183

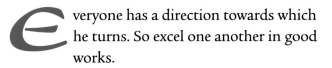veryone has a direction towards which
he turns. So excel one another in good
works.

Al-Baqarah 2:148

DAY
184

pend in the way of God and do not by your own hands throw yourself into destruction, but do good, for God loves those who do good.

Al-Baqarah 2:195

DAY
185

Believers! Fear God and be with those
who are true (in word and deed).

Al-Tawbah 9:119

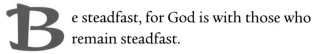 e steadfast, for God is with those who remain steadfast.

Al-Anfal 8:46

DAY
187

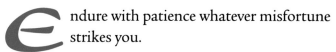

ndure with patience whatever misfortune strikes you.

Luqman 31:17

Those who say: "Our Lord is God" and thereafter remain constant (on the straight path) shall have nothing to fear or grieve. They are the people of Paradise. They shall remain in it forever as a reward for their good works.

Al-Ahqaf 46:13

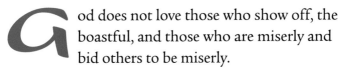 od does not love those who show off, the boastful, and those who are miserly and bid others to be miserly.

Al-Hadid 57:23-24

He who commits a fault or a sin and then blames an innocent person with it, burdens himself with falsehood as well as an open sin.

Al-Nisa' 4:112

DAY
191

 Believers! Do not let your acts of charity go to waste by stressing your own kindness and causing hurt (to those helped by you).

Al-Baqarah 2:264

Do not cast your eyes (with jealousy) towards the worldly goods that God has given to other people.

Al-Hijr 15:88

o not turn your eyes greedily towards the splendour of the worldly life that God has given to other people in order to test them. But the provision of your Lord is better and more enduring.

Ta' Ha' 20: 131

DAY
194

 Believers! Fear God and speak the truth.
God will set your deeds aright and will
forgive you your sins. Whoever obeys
God and His Messenger achieves a great
success.

Al-Ahzab 33:70-71

198

hoever comes with a good deed will get a reward better than it and will be made secure from the terror of the Day of Judgement. But whoever comes with an evil deed will be thrown into the Hellfire. Will you be repaid for anything other than what you have done?

Al-Naml 27:89-90

o the unbelievers take partners (with God), those who cannot create anything? Rather, they themselves are created. And they have no power to help others nor can they help themselves.

Al-A'raf 7:191-192

DAY
197

If there comes to you an evil thought
from Satan, take refuge with God.
He is All Hearing, All-Knowing.

Al-A'raf 7:200

If you repent, it will be for your own good. But if you do not, know well that you cannot escape God.

Al-Tawbah 9:3

DAY
199

Call upon God in fear and hope. God's
mercy is near those who do good.

Al-A'raf 7:56

henever God's clear revelations are recited to those who do not expect to meet God, they say: "Bring us a Qur'an other than this one or at least make changes in it." (O Prophet Muhammad) tell them: "It is not for me to change it of my own will. I only follow what is revealed to me."

Yunus 10:15

DAY
201

God created the heavens and the earth with a purpose so that each person shall be repaid according to his deeds and none shall be wronged.

Al-Jathiyah 45:22

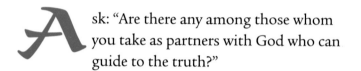sk: "Are there any among those whom you take as partners with God who can guide to the truth?"

Say: "It is God alone Who guides to the truth. Then who deserves to be followed – He Who guides to the truth, or he who cannot find the right way unless he is himself guided? What is wrong with you? How badly you judge!"

Yunus 10:35

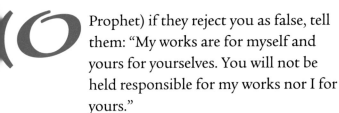

Prophet) if they reject you as false, tell them: "My works are for myself and yours for yourselves. You will not be held responsible for my works nor I for yours."

Yunus 10:41

No one shall bear another's burden.
Man shall have only what he strives for.

Al-Najm 53:38-39

DAY
205

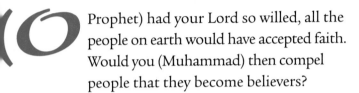 Prophet) had your Lord so willed, all the people on earth would have accepted faith. Would you (Muhammad) then compel people that they become believers?

Yunus 10:99

Can he who follows clear guidance from the Lord be like him whose evil acts are made attractive to him and who is driven by lust?

Muhammad 47:14

DAY
207

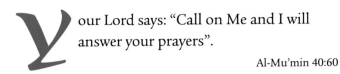

your Lord says: "Call on Me and I will answer your prayers".

Al-Mu'min 40:60

T here is not a single moving creature on earth whose sustenance God is not responsible for. He knows where it lives and its final resting place.

Hud 11:6

DAY
209

s for those who desire only the present world and its joys, God fully repays them for their work in this world. They are made to suffer no decrease in what is their due.

However, they shall have nothing in the Hereafter except Hellfire. (There they shall come to know) that their deeds in the world have come to nothing and that whatever they did is absolutely useless (in the Hereafter).

Hud 11:15-16

DAY
210

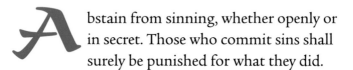
bstain from sinning, whether openly or in secret. Those who commit sins shall surely be punished for what they did.

Al-An'am 6:120

o they not travel in the land that their hearts might understand and their ears might hear? For it is not the eyes that are blind but blinded are the hearts within their breasts.

Al-Hajj 22:46

DAY
212

od sends down water from the sky in right measure, and makes it stay in the earth. God has the power to make it to disappear (as He wishes). Then through this (water) He grows gardens of date-palms and vines for you so that you may have plenty of fruit from which you may eat.

Al-Mu'minun 23:18-19

DAY
213

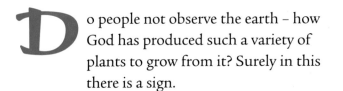

o people not observe the earth – how God has produced such a variety of plants to grow from it? Surely in this there is a sign.

Al-Shu'ara' 26:7-8

DAY
214

For men there is a share in what their parents and relatives leave behind, and for women there is a share in what their parents and relatives leave behind, be it little or much, a share prescribed by God.

Al-Nisa' 4:7

DAY
215

Pray: "My Lord! I take refuge in You from the suggestions of the evil ones. I take refuge in You lest they should approach me."

Al-Mu'minun 23:97

DAY 216

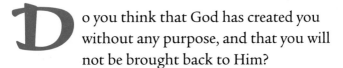

o you think that God has created you without any purpose, and that you will not be brought back to Him?

Al-Mu'minun 23:115

DAY
217

(Let people not forget) the Day of Judgement when their own tongues, their hands, and their feet shall bear witness against them regarding what they used to do.

Al-Nur 24:24

DAY
218

od is well aware of your condition. On the Day of Judgement when people will return to Him, He will tell them all what they did for God knows everything.

Al-Nur 24:64

DAY
219

If the wrongdoers possessed all the treasures of the earth and as much besides, they would gladly offer this on the Day of Judgement to save themselves from terrible punishment.

Al-Zumar 39:47

Think about him who has taken his base desires for his god! Can you (O Prophet) take responsibility for him (in guiding him to the right way)? Do you think that most of them hear or understand? For they are merely like cattle – no, they are even further astray (from the right path).

Al-Furqan 25:43-44

DAY
221

I t is God Who has joined the two seas: one sweet and palatable and the other salty and bitter; and He has set a barrier and an unsurpassable barrier between the two that keeps them apart.

Al-Furqan 25:53

DAY 222

(T)he true servants of the Merciful God are) those who are neither extravagant nor miserly in their spending. They follow the golden mean between the two.

Al-Furqan 25:67

Indeed there is a lesson for you in cattle. God provides you with drink out of what they have in bellies and you have many other benefits in them. You eat of them and are carried on them and also on ships.

Al-Mu'minun 23:21-22

Nothing will help man on the Day of Judgement, neither his wealth nor his children. Only he who brings to God a sound heart will achieve success.

Al-Shu'ara' 26:88

DAY
225

y Lord! Keep me under Your control so that I may give thanks for the favours which You have done to me and to my parents and that I act piously in a manner that would please You. Include me, out of Your mercy, among Your pious servants."

Al-Naml 27:19

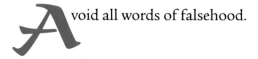void all words of falsehood.

Al-Hajj 22:30

DAY
227

he believers will be granted their reward twice over because they remained consistent all along. They repel evil with good and spend (in charity) out of the sustenance that God has given them. When they hear any vain talk, they turn away from it, saying: "We have our acts and you have yours. Peace be upon you. We do not want to act like the people of ignorance."

Al-Qasas 28:54-55

DAY
228

hatever you have been given is a provision for the life of this world and its glitter. Yet that which is with God is much better and long lasting. Do you not use your intellect?

Al-Qasas 28: 60

DAY
229

He who brings a good deed will be rewarded with what is better, but those who bring evil deeds will not be punished more than for what they did.

Al-Qasas 28:84

 hoever works hard (in the cause of God) does so to his own good. Certainly God does not stand in need of anyone in the whole of creation.

Al-'Ankabut 29:6

DAY
231

Wrongdoers are friends of one another while God is the friend of those who fear Him.

Al-Jathiyah 45:19

DAY
232

oday all good things are made lawful for you. The food of the People of the Book (i.e. the Jews and Christians) is permitted to you and your food to them.

Al-Ma'idah 5:5

DAY
233

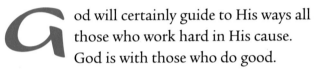

od will certainly guide to His ways all those who work hard in His cause. God is with those who do good.

Al-'Ankabut 29:69

DAY
234

n the Day of Judgement when the Hour will come, the wicked shall swear that they had stayed (in the world) no more than an hour. Thus they used to deceive themselves.

Al-Rum 30:55

He who gives thanks to God does so to his own good. And one who disbelieves (let him realize that) God is Independent, Most Praiseworthy.

Luqman 31:12

He who surrenders himself to God and leads a pious life gets hold of the most firm handle. The final decision of all matters rests with God.

Luqman 31:22

God's is the kingdom of the heavens and the earth. On the Day when the Hour of Judgement shall come, the followers of falsehood shall be in total loss.

Al-Jathiyah 45:27

nly those believe in God's signs are they who when they are given good advice through God's verses, fall down prostrate and celebrate the praises of their Lord and are not given to pride. Their limbs forsake their beds of sleep, and they call upon their Lord in fear and hope, and spend in charity out of the sustenance granted to them by God.

Al-Sajdah 32:15-16

DAY 239

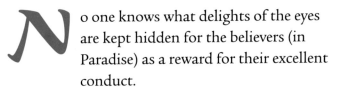

o one knows what delights of the eyes are kept hidden for the believers (in Paradise) as a reward for their excellent conduct.

Al-Sajdah 32:17

ho is more unjust than he who is given
good advice through the signs of the
Lord and yet he turns away from them?
Surely God will fully punish these
wrongdoers.

Al-Sajdah 32:22

 Prophet) say: "My Lord grants provision in plenty to whom He wills and restricts it for whom He pleases. Whatever you spend (in charity), He will replace it. Surely, He is the Best of Providers."

Saba' 34:39

 people, bring to mind God's favours upon you. Is there any creator, apart from God, who provides you with your sustenance out of the heavens and the earth?

Fatir 35:3

 people, God's promise is certainly true. So let the life of this world not deceive you and let not the deceiver (Satan) deceive you about God. Surely Satan is your enemy. He calls his followers to his way so that they may be among the people of Hellfire.

Fatir 35:5-6

No one shall bear another's burden. If one who is heavily burdened calls another to carry his load, none of it shall be carried by the other, even though he may be a close relative.

Fatir 35:18

Let the dead earth be a sign for people. God gives it life and produces grain from it, which they eat. God makes in the earth gardens of date-palms and vines and He causes rivers to flow.

Ya' Sin 36:33

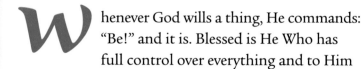

Whenever God wills a thing, He commands: "Be!" and it is. Blessed is He Who has full control over everything and to Him you all shall return.

Ya' Sin 36:82-83

DAY
247

od's severe punishment awaits those who stray from His path, for they forgot the Day of Judgement.

Sad 38:26

DAY
248

od did not create the heavens and the
earth and all that lies between them in
vain: this is the fancy of only those who
deny the truth.

Sad 38:27

n excellent abode awaits those who fear God – everlasting gardens with gates wide open for them. There they shall rest and ask for fruits and drinks in plenty. There they shall be with well-matched, coy spouses. All this is what you are promised on the Day of Judgement. This is God's provision for you, which will never end.

Sad 38:49-54

*J*f you disbelieve, know well that God has no need of you. Yet He does not like unbelief in His servants.

Al-Zumar 39:7

DAY
251

حose who are steadfast shall be granted
their reward beyond all measure.

Al-Zumar 39:10

od presents a parable: there is a slave owned by several quarrelsome masters, each claiming that slave for himself. And there is another who is exclusively owned by one master. Can the two be alike?

Al-Zumar 39:29

DAY
253

He who follows the right way does so to his own benefit and he who goes astray shall hurt only himself by straying.

Al-Zumar 39:41

257

DAY
254

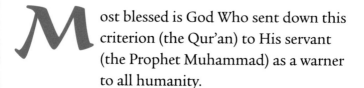

ost blessed is God Who sent down this
criterion (the Qur'an) to His servant
(the Prophet Muhammad) as a warner
to all humanity.

Al-Furqan 25:1

DAY
255

urn to your Lord and surrender yourselves to Him before the punishment
overtakes you, for then you shall not
receive any help.

Al-Zumar 39:54

Those who avoid disobeying their Lord will be escorted in groups to Paradise. When they arrive there, its gates will have already been thrown open and its keepers will welcome them thus: "Peace be upon you. You have done well. So enter and you shall live in it forever."

Al-Zumar 39:73

DAY
257

God knows even the stealthiest glance of the eyes and all the secrets that the hearts conceal.

Al-Mu'min 40:19

DAY
258

Be steadfast. God's promise is true. Ask God for forgiveness of your mistakes and celebrate the praise of your Lord, every evening and morning.

Al-Mu'min 40:55

DAY
259

Those who have faith and do good,
they shall have a never-ending reward.

Ha'. Mim. Al-Sajdah 41:8

There is no blame upon him who avenges himself after he has been wronged. Blame falls only upon those who wrong people and commit excesses on earth. A painful punishment awaits them. Yet he who patiently endures and forgives, it is conduct of great resolve.

Al-Shura 42:41-43

DAY
261

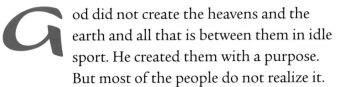

od did not create the heavens and the earth and all that is between them in idle sport. He created them with a purpose. But most of the people do not realize it.

Al-Dukhan 44:38-39

he Day of Judgement is the appointed time for everyone. On that Day a friend shall be of no help to a friend. Nor shall any be helped, except those on whom God has mercy. He is the Most Mighty, Most Compassionate.

Al-Dukhan 44:40-42

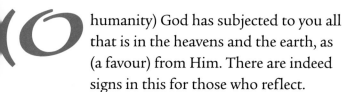

humanity) God has subjected to you all that is in the heavens and the earth, as (a favour) from Him. There are indeed signs in this for those who reflect.

Al-Jathiyah 45:13

he example of those who take anyone other than God as their protector is like that of a spider that builds a house. However, the frailest of all houses is the spider's, if they but knew it.

Al-'Ankabut 29: 41

od originates creation and will revive it again. How then are you being misled?

Yunus 10:34

Consider the case of one who took his desires as his god and then God caused him to go astray despite his knowledge, and sealed his hearing and his heart, and put a covering over his sight? Who other than God can direct him to the right way? Will you not take this to heart?

Al-Jathiyah 45:23

ell them (O Prophet): "It is God Who gives you life and then causes you to die. He it is Who will bring you all back together on the Day of Judgement, about which there is no doubt."

Al-Jathiyah 45:26

od alone has the knowledge of the Last Hour. It is He Who sends down rain and knows what is in the wombs. No person knows what he will earn tomorrow. Nor does he know in which land he will die. God alone is All-Knowing, All-Aware.

Luqman 31:34

n the Day of Judgement you will see all people fallen upon their knees. They shall be summoned to come forth and see the record of their deeds. They will be told: "Today you shall be repaid for your acts. This is Our (God's) record which bears witness against you with truth. God used to record all that you did."

Al-Jathiyah 45:28-29

n the Day of Judgement) the evil of their works will become clear to evil-doers and what they made mockery of will surround them, and it will be said: "God will forget you today as you forgot your meeting on this Day. The Hellfire shall now be your abode and you shall have no one to come to your aid."

Al-Jathiyah 45:33-34

 Believers! Why do you preach that which you do not practise? It is most hateful in the sight of God that you preach what you do not practise.

Al-Saff 61:2-3

od gave them (the unbelievers) ears, eyes and hearts. But nothing helped them — neither their ears nor their eyes nor their hearts. For they denied the signs of God. What they mock at shall surround them.

Al-Ahqaf 46:26

Prophet) say: "Truth has come to you from your Lord. Whoever then follows true guidance does so for his own good; and whoever strays, his straying shall be to his own loss."

Yunus 10:108

Y ou are those who are called upon to spend in God's way. But some of you are miserly. Whoever is miserly is in fact miserly with himself, for God is All-Sufficient whereas you stand in need of Him.

Muhammad 47:38

DAY
275

God does not wrong people, but they wrong themselves.

Yunus 10:44

od has created everything in proportion and due measure. His command consists only of a single word which is carried out in the blink of an eye.

Al-Qamar 54:49-50

The life of this world is nothing but a delusion. Compete with one another in seeking your Lord's forgiveness and a Paradise that is as wide as the heavens and the earth.

Al-Hadid 57:20-21

DAY

278

Those who are safe against their own greed, they are the ones who shall prosper.

Al-Hashr 59:9

believers, fear God and let every person
look to what he sends forward for the
Next Life. Fear God, for He is fully aware
of all that you do.

Al-Hashr 59:18

The death from which you flee will certainly overtake you. Then you shall return to God Who knows fully all that is hidden and evident. Then He will inform you all that you used to do.

Al-Jumu'ah 62:8

DAY
281

God created the heavens and the earth with a purpose and gave you your excellent forms. To Him is your ultimate return. He knows what is in the heavens and the earth, and knows what you conceal and what you reveal. He even knows what lies hidden in the breasts of people.

Al-Taghabun 64:3-4

Whoever fears God, He will remove his evil deeds, and will increase his reward.

Al-Talaq 65:5

God created life and death so that He might try you as to (show) which of you is better in conduct. He is the Most Mighty, Most Forgiving.

Al-Mulk 67:2

DAY
284

You cannot find any lack of proportion in the creation of the Most Gracious God. Look again: can you see any flaw? Again look, and then again, and in the end your vision will come back to you tired and frustrated.

Al-Mulk 67:3-4

hether you speak in secrecy or **openly,**
(it is all the same to God). He **even knows**
the secrets that lie hidden **in the breasts**
of people. Should He not **know what** He
has created? He is All-**Subtle, All**-Aware.

Al-Mulk 67:13-14

DAY
286

(O)n the Day of Judgement) no friend will enquire about any of his friends, though they shall be in the sight of one another. The guilty one would like to save himself by offering his children, spouse, brother and relatives who had stood by him, and all the persons of the earth, if only he could thereby save himself.

Al-Ma'arij 70:10-14

DAY
287

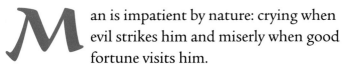

Man is impatient by nature: crying when evil strikes him and miserly when good fortune visits him.

Al-Ma'arij 70:19-21

DAY
288

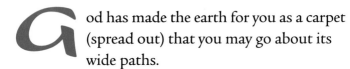

God has made the earth for you as a carpet (spread out) that you may go about its wide paths.

Nuh 71:19-20

If you persist in disbelieving, how will you save yourself against (the misery of) the Day of Judgement that shall even turn children grey-haired?

Al-Muzammil 73:17

oes man imagine that God will not be able to bring his bones together again? Yes, indeed, God has the power to re-create even his fingertips.

Al-Qiyamah 75:3-4

od created man out of a drop of inter-
mingled sperm so that He might try
him. God gave him hearing and sight
and showed him the right path. Whether
he chooses to be thankful or unthankful
(to his Lord rests upon his own free will).

Al-Dahr 76:2-3

He who fears to stand (on the Day of Judgement) before the Lord and keeps himself away from evil desires, surely his abode shall be Paradise.

al-Nazi'at 79:40

DAY
293

o you know what the Day of Judgement is? It is the Day when no one shall have the power to do anything for anyone and all command shall only be God's.

Al-Infitar 82:18-19

oe to those who deal in fraud! Who, when they receive their due from others, demand their full share, but when they weigh or measure for others, they give less than what is due.

Al-Mutaffifin 83:1-3

od created everything for the first time
and it is He Who will create it again. He
is the All-Forgiving, All-Loving Lord of
the glorious Throne, Who does whatever
He wills.

Al-Buruj 85:13-16

Let man consider of what he was created. He was created of a gushing fluid, emanating from between the loins and the ribs. Surely God has the power to bring man back (to life in the Hereafter).

Al-Tariq 86:5-8

DAY
297

n the Day of Judgement man will realize (the truth), but what good will that understanding be? He will say: "Would that I had done good that would have helped me in the Afterlife."

Al-Fajr 89:23-24

hose who fear God will be kept away from the Hellfire. For they spend their wealth in order to purify themselves, not as payment for any favours received by them. They spend only to gain the pleasure of their Lord, Most High. God will surely be well-pleased with them.

Al-Layl 92:17-21

 people,) the desire for more and more worldly gains and to outdo others in this regard keep you occupied until you reach your graves.

Al-Takathur 102:1-2

S urely your Lord will repay everyone in full for their acts, for He is well aware of all that they do.

Hud 11:111

DAY
301

Your Lord would never wrongfully destroy the towns while those living in them are pious.

Hud 11:117

DAY
302

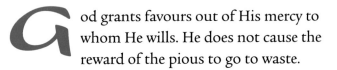

God grants favours out of His mercy to whom He wills. He does not cause the reward of the pious to go to waste.

Yusuf 12:56

DAY
303

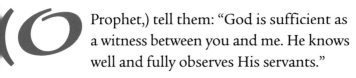

(O Prophet,) tell them: "God is sufficient as a witness between you and me. He knows well and fully observes His servants."

Bani Isra'il 17:96

DAY
304

Wealth and children are a passing enjoyment of this worldly life. But works of lasting goodness are best in the sight of your Lord for reward and are a better source of hope.

Al-Kahf 18:46

In the stories of earlier people there is a lesson for people of understanding. What is described in the Qur'an is no invention. Rather, it is confirmation of the heavenly Books that came before it. In it is a detailed explanation of everything, and guidance and mercy for the people who have faith.

Yusuf 12:111

God does not change the condition of a people unless they change what is in themselves.

Al-Ra'd 13:11

To God alone all prayers should be addressed, for those whom people address in their prayers besides God are totally powerless to answer them.

Al-Ra'd 13:14

There is a good reward for those who accept the message of their Lord. For those who do not, (a time will come when) they will offer all that they have. However, even if they had all the wealth of the world and twice as much to save themselves (from the punishment of God), it would not be accepted.

Al-Ra'd 13:18

Paradise shall be the final abode of those who fulfil their pledge to God and do not break it after having firmly confirmed it. They maintain the ties (of relationship) which God has ordered to be joined. They fear their Lord and dread lest they are subjected to a harsh trial. They are consistent in seeking the pleasure of their Lord, establish Prayer and spend both privately and publicly out of the wealth given to them by God. They repel evil with good.

Al-Ra'd 13:20-22

DAY
310

The unbelievers celebrate much the life of the world, but when compared with the Next Life, the life of the world is no more than a passing enjoyment.

Al-Ra'd 13:26

DAY
311

hose who believe (in the message of truth) and do good are certain to attain happiness and a joyful end.

Al-Ra'd 13:29

DAY
312

God will judge and no one has the power
to alter His judgement. He is swift in
taking account.

Al-Ra'd 13:41

o you not consider the parable of the good word as related by God? A good word is like a good tree, whose root is firmly fixed and whose branches reach the sky, always bearing fruit in every season with the permission of its Lord. God gives examples to humanity that they may take them to heart. The parable of an evil word is that of an evil tree, uprooted from the surface of the earth, and unable to survive.

Ibrahim 14:24-26

DAY
314

Were you to count the favours of God, you will never be able to count them. However, man is unjust and utterly ungrateful.

Ibrahim 14:34

DAY
315

Do not think that God is unaware of the evil acts in which evil-doers are engaged. He is only granting them respite until the Day of Judgement when their eyes will stare in horror.

Ibrahim 14:42

 Prophet!) Warn people of the Day of Judgement when the heavens and the earth shall be changed altogether. All will appear then fully exposed before God, the One, the Supreme.

Ibrahim 14:48

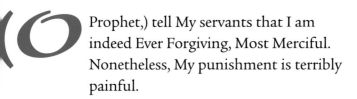

(O Prophet,) tell My servants that I am indeed Ever Forgiving, Most Merciful. Nonetheless, My punishment is terribly painful.

Al-Hijr 15:49

DAY
318

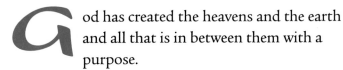

od has created the heavens and the earth and all that is in between them with a purpose.

Al-Hijr 15:85

DAY
319

Jn the numerous things of various colours that God has created for you on earth, there are signs for those who reflect.

Al-Nahl 16:13

DAY
320

 s for the possibility (of the Day of Judgement) remember that when God wills
something, He has to only say: "Be" and
it is.

Al-Nahl 16:40

ood fortune in this world awaits those who do good. Certainly the abode of the Hereafter is even better for them. How excellent is the abode of those who fear God! They shall be admitted to everlasting gardens beneath which rivers flow. There they shall have all that they desire. Thus God does reward those who fear Him.

Al-Nahl 16:30-31

ere God to take people to task for their wrongdoing, He would not have spared even a single creature on the face of the earth. However, He grants them respite until an appointed term. When that term arrives, they will have no power to delay or to advance it even by a single moment.

Al-Nahl 16:61

urely there is a lesson for you in cattle. God provides you with a drink which is in their bellies, between their excreta and blood — pure milk which is a delicious drink for those who take it.

Al-Nahl 16:66

DAY 324

od has blessed you with spouses from your own species and through them has granted you children and grandchildren. He has also provided you with wholesome things as sustenance. (Even in the face of all this) do people still believe in falsehood and deny God's bounties?

Al-Nahl 16:72

od brought you forth from your mothers' wombs when you knew nothing and then blessed you with hearing, sight and thinking hearts so that you might give thanks (to God).

Al-Nahl 16:78

DAY
326

Whatever you have will certainly pass away. However, whatever is with God will endure. God shall give those who are patient their reward according to the best of their acts.

Al-Nahl 16:96

 hosoever does good – man or woman –
and has faith, God will surely grant
them a good life and will reward them
according to the best of their works.

Al-Nahl 16:97

The (Egyptian) magicians (after their defeat by the Prophet Moses) told Pharaoh: "By God Who has created us, we shall never prefer you to the truth after clear signs have been seen by us. So give orders whatever you will. Your orders will apply, at the most, to the present life of this world. We believe in our Lord that He may forgive us our sins and also forgive us for the use of magic into which you had forced us. God is best and He alone will live forever."

Ta' Ha' 20:72-73

God is Much Forgiving, Most Merciful to those who do some evil out of ignorance but who then repent and make amends.

Al-Nahl 16:119

he Qur'an guides humanity to the straight path. To those who believe in it and do good, it gives the good news that a great reward awaits them. It warns those who do not believe in the Hereafter that God has prepared a painful punishment for them.

Bani Isra'il 17:9

They ask: "When we are reduced to bones and particles of dust, will we be raised again as a new creation?" Tell them: "(You will be raised again even if) you turn into stone or iron or any other form of creation which you think are the hardest of all (from which to create again). They ask: "Who will bring us back to life?" Tell them: "God Who created you in the first place."

Bani Isra'il 17:51

Prophet,) tell My servants: "They should always say that which is best. It is Satan who causes differences among people. Satan is indeed an open enemy to all humanity."

Bani Isra'il 17:53

od honoured the children of Adam, bore them across land and sea and provided them with good things for their sustenance. He has exalted them above many of His creatures.

Bani Isra'il 17:70

DAY
334

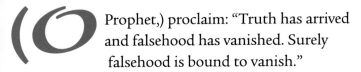

(O Prophet,) proclaim: "Truth has arrived
and falsehood has vanished. Surely
falsehood is bound to vanish."

Bani Isra'il 17:81

God has explained things for people in this Qur'an in many ways to help them understand God's message. Yet most of the people knowingly persist in unbelief.

Bani Isra'il 17:89

DAY
336

God does not allow the reward of those
people who fear God and remain patient
to go to waste.

Yusuf 12:90

DAY
337

od has sent down the Qur'an with truth.
It has descended with the truth. God has
sent you (O Prophet) to proclaim good
news and to warn people.

Bani Isra'il 17:105

ay: "All praise be to God Who has neither taken to Himself a son, nor has He any partner in His kingdom, and nor does He need anyone out of any weakness to protect Him. So praise Him in a manner befitting His glory."

Bani Isra'il 17:111

od has made all that is on earth an attraction in order to test people as to which of them is better is conduct. Eventually God will reduce all that is on earth to a barren plain.

Al-Kahf 18:8

D o you seek the pomp and glitter of this world? Do not follow him whose heart God has caused to be negligent of His remembrance and who blindly follows his desires and goes beyond all limits.

Al-Kahf 18:28

s for those who believe and do good, God will not let their reward be lost. They shall live in eternal gardens beneath which rivers flow. They will be adorned there with bracelets of gold. They will be dressed in green garments of silk and rich brocade and will rest on raised couches. How excellent is their reward and how fair their resting place!

Al-Kahf 18:30-31

DAY
342

Many are the signs in the heavens and the earth which people pass by without paying attention.

Yusuf 12:105

he record of people's acts will be placed
before them and you will see the guilty
full of fear for what is contains. They
will exclaim: "Woe to us! What a record
this is! It leaves out nothing, big or small.
It contains everything." They will find
their own works confronting them.
Your Lord does not wrong anyone.

Al-Kahf 18:49

DAY
344

God has explained things to people in the Qur'an in several ways, using all sorts of parables. However, humanity is too contentious.

Al-Kahf 18:54

ho is more wicked than that person who, when he is reminded by the revelations of his Lord, turns away from them and forgets (the consequences) of the works of his own hands?

Al-Kahf 18:57

Those admitted to Paradise shall not hear in it anything vain. They shall hear there only what is good. They shall have their provision in it, morning and evening. Such is Paradise which God will grant to those of His servants who are God-fearing.

Maryam 19:62

Humanity often asks: "Will I be raised to life after I die?" Does man not realize that God created him when he was nothing?

Maryam 19:66-67

God increases in guidance those who follow the right way. Good acts of lasting value are better in the sight of your Lord for bringing reward and for a better end.

Maryam 19:76

The unbelievers have taken other gods besides the One True God so that they may be a source of strength for them. By no means! They (the false gods) shall deny their worship and shall become their enemies instead (on the Day of Judgement).

Maryam 19:81-82

he Day shall come soon when God will
bring together the God-fearing people
as honoured guests to Himself, the Most
Compassionate Lord. He shall drive the
guilty ones as a thirsty herd to Hell.

Maryam 19:85

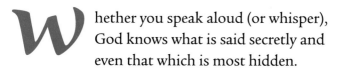

Whether you speak aloud (or whisper), God knows what is said secretly and even that which is most hidden.

Ta' Ha' 20:7

DAY
352

The Hour of Judgement is approaching. However, God has kept its time of coming a secret so that everyone may be repaid in accordance with his works.

Ta' Ha' 20:15

DAY
353

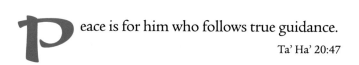

Peace is for him who follows true guidance.

Ta' Ha' 20:47

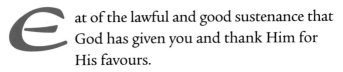

at of the lawful and good sustenance that God has given you and thank Him for His favours.

Al-Nahl 16:114

he truth is that Hell awaits him who comes to his Lord, burdened with sins: he shall neither die in it nor live. However, he who comes to Him with faith and good works shall be raised to a high rank. He shall live forever in eternal gardens beneath which rivers flow. Such will be the reward of those who purify themselves.

Ta' Ha' 20:75-76

DAY
356

God is Most Forgiving to him who repents and believes, does good and follows the right way.

Ta' Ha' 20:82

Command your family to offer prayer and to keep offering it. God does not ask you for any worldly things. Rather, it is God Who provides for you and the pious shall have the best end (in the Hereafter).

Ta' Ha' 20:132

The time of people's judgement has drawn near yet they turn away, utterly neglectful. When a fresh warning comes to them from their Lord, they remain neglectful and lost in vain things as their hearts are set upon other concerns.

Al-Anbiya' 21:1

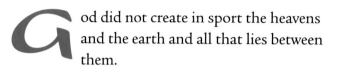

God did not create in sport the heavens and the earth and all that lies between them.

Al-Anbiya' 21:16

DAY
360

ad there been any gods in the heavens and the earth apart from the One True God, there would have been total chaos in the heavens and the earth. Glory be to God, the Lord of the Throne, Who is far above their (unbelievers') false descriptions of Him.

Al-Anbiya' 21:22

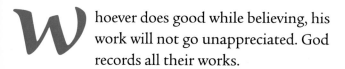

hoever does good while believing, his work will not go unappreciated. God records all their works.

Al-Anbiya' 21:94

od brings you forth as babies and nurtures you so that you may come of age. Among you is one who dies (young) and another who is kept back to a most advanced age, so that, after having gained knowledge, he reaches a stage when he knows nothing.

Al-Hajj 22:5

e devoted only to God, taking no one other than Him as God. Whoever does so, it is as though he fell down from the sky and that either birds snatched him away, or the wind swept him to a distant place (causing him to be shattered to pieces).

Al-Hajj 22:31

(O Prophet,) give good news to those who humble themselves before God, whose hearts tremble whenever God is mentioned, who patiently bear with every difficulty, who establish Prayer and who spend (on good causes) out of what God has given them.

Al-Hajj 22:34-35

 od has subjected the animals to you that you may give thanks. Neither their flesh nor their blood reaches God (as you sacrifice them for Him). It is only your piety that reaches Him. He has subjected the animals (to you) so that you may proclaim God's praises for the guidance with which He has blessed you.

Al-Hajj 22:36-37

SELECT QUR'ANIC PRAYERS

The Qur'an has directed the believers to address their prayers to God. Contained in the Qur'an are several prayers which God taught to the Prophets and to the believers in general. A selection of these appears below:

"O our Lord, give us good in this world and in the Hereafter. Save us from the Hellfire."

Al-Baqarah 2:201

"O our Lord, turn the punishment of Hell away from us, for its punishment is indeed terrible."

Al-Furqan 25:65

"O our Lord, grant us spouses and children to be the joy in our eyes, and make us the leaders of the pious."

Al-Furqan 25:74

"O our Lord, cover us with Your forgiveness – me, my parents and all believers on the Day of Judgement."

Ibrahim 14:41

"O my Lord, I am in need of any good that You may send me."

Al-Qasas 28:24

"O my Lord, increase me in knowledge."

Ta' Ha' 20:114

INDEX OF QUR'ANIC PASSAGES

The Qur'anic Passage	Day of Year
Al-Hajj 22:5	362
Al-Hajj 22:30	226
Al-Hajj 22:31	363
Al-Hajj 22:34-35	364
Al-Hajj 22:36-37	365
Al-Hajj 22:40	164
Al-Hajj 22:46	211
Al-Hajj 22:73	31
Ha'. Mim. Al-Sajdah 41:8	259
Ha'. Mim. Al-Sajdah 41:34	24
Al-Hashr 59:9	278
Al-Hashr 59:18	279
Al-Hashr 59:19	156
Al-Hijr 15:49	317
Al-Hijr 15:85	318
Al-Hijr 15:88	192
Hud 11:4	163
Hud 11:6	208
Hud 11:15-16	209
Hud 11:111	300
Hud 11:113	176
Hud 11:117	301
Hud 11:123	101
Al-Hujurat 49:6	130
Al-Hujurat 49:11	71
Al-Hujurat 49:12	70
Al-Hujurat 49:13	1
Al-Humazah 104:1-4	89
Ibrahim 14:1	106
Ibrahim 14:24-26	313
Ibrahim 14:34	314

379

SUBJECT INDEX

References are to the days of the year, not to page numbers.

Also available from Kube Publishing

Daily Wisdom
Sayings of the Prophet Muhammad ﷺ

Abdur Raheem Kidwai

This popular companion volume to
Daily Wisdom: Selections from the Holy Qur'an
is a beautiful presentation of the Prophet's
teachings that engages the reader in a
moment of daily reflection, soul-searching
and self-realisation. With 365 traditions
covering the whole year, this is a must for
every home.

Abdur Raheem Kidwai is Professor of English
at the Aligarh Muslim University, Aligarh,
India and a prolific author. He has published
extensively on the English translations of the
Qur'an, literary Orientalism, English studies
and Urdu literature.

400pages, ISBN 978-1-84774-018-2 casebound